STARTING ECOLOGY

Wood

Written and
photographed by

Colin S.Milkins

Artist: Sarah Beatty

Wayland

STARTING ECOLOGY

Pond and Stream

Seashore

Wasteland

Wood

Editor: Sarah Doughty

First published in 1993
by Wayland (Publishers) Ltd
61 Western Road, Hove,
East Sussex, BN3 1JD, England

British Library Cataloguing in Publication Data
Milkins, Colin S.
Wood. - (Starting Ecology Series)
I. Title II. Series
574.5

ISBN 0 7502 0821 X

Typeset by Dorchester Typesetting Group Ltd, England
Printed in Belgium by Casterman S.A.

What is ecology?

Ecology is the study of the way plants and animals live together in a habitat. A scientist who studies this is called an ecologist. An ecologist finds out about a habitat by observing the area and carrying out experiments. If you do the projects in this book, you will be an ecologist too.

Always go to woodland areas as a group with a parent or teacher, and never wander off on your own.

CONTENTS

The words in **bold** are explained
in the glossary on page 30.

What is a wood?

A wood is made up of trees. Woodland once covered most of Britain. A squirrel could have crossed from one side of the country to the other by jumping from tree to tree. Today only a small part of Britain is made up of woodland areas.

Trees are not the only plants that grow in a wood. Shrubs often grow under the trees. In some woods there is also a layer of **herbs** that grows close to the ground.

Many animals have their homes in woodland areas, and feed on the plants that grow there.

◀ *Pine forests can be very dark. The sun cannot get through the thick canopy.*

Woodlands are not the same in all areas. This is because different types of trees and plants grow better on different types of soil. Silver birch and Scot's pine trees grow well on sandy soils and oak trees grow better on clay.

▲ *Light is very important to things living in woodlands.*

Some woods let in more light than others. A thick **canopy** of leaves will make a wood shady. Some woods are wetter because more rain falls, or the soil holds more water. This means that the animals that live in the woodland and feed on the plants will be different too.

Find out what the woodland is like in your area and which plants and animals live there.

▶ *The primrose is a woodland herb that flowers early in spring.*

Looking at leaves

Ash leaf

Scot's pine leaf

All trees have different shaped leaves. You can learn to recognize trees by looking at the sort of leaves they have. The pictures on these two pages show leaves from a number of different trees.

Some of the leaves are made up of only one part. They are called simple leaves. The others are made up of separate leaflets and are called compound leaves.

Learn the names of leaves by playing 'name the leaf game'. Find some leaves from oak, ash, hazel, sweet chestnut, silver birch and Scot's pine trees. Stick them on to a chart. Label your leaves a, b, c, d, e and f.

Next make some leaf description cards. Write the name of the leaf at the top of the card. Then write a description of the leaf. Use the questions below to guide you.

1. Is the leaf made of one or several leaflets?
2. Is the leaf broad, or thin like a needle?
3. What colour is the topside of the leaf?
4. What colour is the underside of the leaf?
5. Are the edges smooth, wavy or toothed like a saw?

When you have finished writing your card, give it to a friend. Ask him or her to look at the leaves on your chart.

See if your friend can name the leaves using your leaf description cards.

Oak leaf

Sweet chestnut leaf

Hazel leaf

Silver birch leaf

▼ *Children playing 'name the leaf' game.*

How living things feed

All living things need food to grow and stay healthy. Most living things eat by taking food into their bodies. But green plants are different. They make their own food in their leaves.

To make food, plants need three things. These are carbon dioxide (a gas in the air), sunlight and water.

The green part of the leaves uses sunlight to change carbon dioxide and water into food for the plant. Carbon dioxide passes into the plant through little holes on the underside of the leaves. The plant uses its roots to get water from the soil. The water then travels up the stem to the leaves, where the food is made.

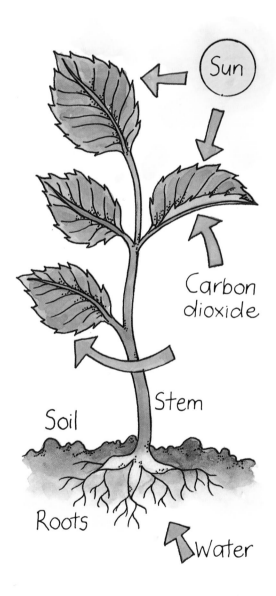

Sun

Carbon dioxide

Stem

Soil

Roots

Water

Plants need sunlight, water and carbon dioxide to make food.

Plants pass on their energy to animals through a **food chain**. Plants are always at the beginning of a food chain. They are eaten by animals who then in turn may be eaten themselves.

The seeds of a plant are eaten by a chaffinch. The chaffinch in turn is eaten by a **bird of prey** such as a sparrowhawk. The energy from the seeds ends up in the sparrowhawk.

Try to draw a diagram showing such a food chain. Here is an example below:

▲ *The green part of leaves makes food for the plant.*

▼ *A food chain. The grass seeds are eaten by the field mouse and the field mouse is eaten by the fox.*

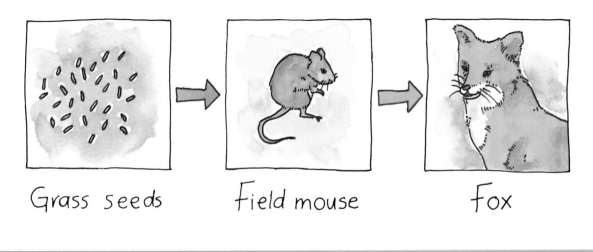

Grass seeds   Field mouse   Fox

Blue tits and pyramids

A common bird found in and around woodland is the blue tit. Blue tits can often be seen in spring looking for juicy caterpillars which they feed to their young. Blue tits are called **predators** because they catch other animals for food. The caterpillars they catch are called their **prey**.

This blue tit is feeding a caterpillar to its chicks.

If your school or home is near a wood, you could put up a nest box for blue tits to nest in. When you hear faint twittering sounds coming from the nest box, the chicks have hatched. A blue tit usually has about ten chicks. This is called its brood size.

You can watch the birds feeding their young, but stay about 15 metres away.

Count the number of caterpillars the parents feed to their young by counting the number of times the birds visit the nest box. They usually feed one caterpillar at a time.

Make a note of each visit for thirty minutes, marking the caterpillars off in tens. How many whole sets of ten caterpillars have you counted?

Now make a chart of your results like the one below on the right. The number of predators and prey are shown as a pyramid. The sets of ten caterpillars are at the bottom of the pyramid, and the sets of ten blue tits are at the top.

Your pyramid is for 30 minutes only. What would it be like after one or two hours of feeding?

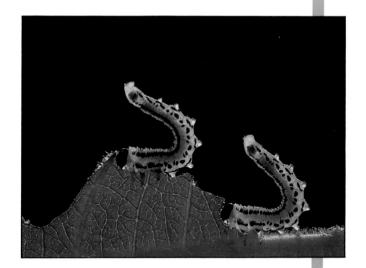

▲ *These caterpillars are the food of blue tits.*

▼ *A pyramid showing predators and prey.*

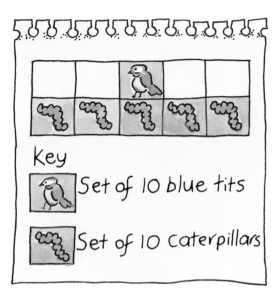

Leaf mines

▲ *A blotch mine on a silver birch leaf.*

▼ *Can you see the caterpillar in this blotch mine? Find its head and six little legs.*

Caterpillars are the young of butterflies and moths. They are long worm-like creatures that usually eat plants. The caterpillars of one type of tiny moth make a pattern on the leaves they eat. You can look for these leaves on trees in the wood.

The caterpillars burrow between the outer layers of the leaf, eating the middle layer as they go. Their burrowing makes a pattern on the leaf, called a mine. Some mines are all wriggly like a snake. These are called **serpentine** mines. They can be found on bramble and silver birch leaves. Other types of mine are just brown patches. These patches are called blotch mines.

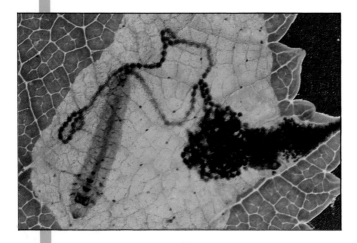

In April, find a low branch of a silver birch tree. Measure one metre along the branch starting at its tip.

Count all of the leaves along this length. Then count them again, this time counting only the mined leaves. Do this with at least five branches. Make a note of the number of leaves and mined leaves.

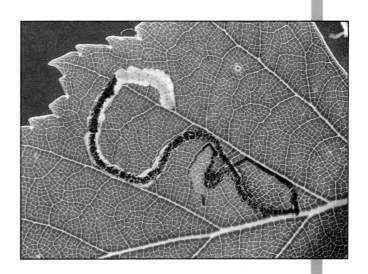

▲ *A serpentine mine. Can you see the caterpillar?*

Show what you have found as a bar graph, even if you did not find any mined leaves. Wait until July and do this project again on the same branches. Does the number of mined leaves change from April to July? If it does, can you think of reasons why?

▶ *On your chart, has the number of mined leaves changed from April to July?*

April   July

This shows the number of mined leaves

This shows the total number of leaves

Rotting leaves

In the spring, woodland plants begin to grow again and make new leaves and flowers after their winter rest. In order to grow, plants need **nutrients** from the soil. When old leaves fall off the trees in autumn, they slowly start to break down in the soil. Their nutrients go back into the soil and are taken up and used by plants again.

In the soil, leaves are broken down and eaten by woodlice and earthworms. **Fungi** and **bacteria** break down the leaves even further. Some leaves break down very quickly when buried in the earth.

◄ *Fungi, like these toadstools, help break down leaves when they fall off the trees in autumn.*

Other types of leaves break down more slowly, because they are very **acidic**. This stops the leaves from rotting quickly. Living things in the soil cannot easily break down the leaves into the nutrients that help other plants to grow. You can carry out an experiment to study how quickly leaves rot.

In September, bury some pine needles and silver birch leaves in moist soil in a container. Make sure it has a lid to stop the soil drying out.

▲ *Bury some silver birch leaves and pine needles in September.*

Next July, carefully remove the soil. Look at the leaves you buried. Which have rotted the most – the pine needles or the silver birch leaves?

▶ *Worms pull leaves into their holes and eat them.*

Mini beasts

▲ *These snake millipedes are mating.*

▼ *The large front legs of this centipede are used to poison prey.*

When visiting woodland, it is fun to look under logs for mini beasts. Look for the black snake millipede which feeds on dead leaves. The centipede may also be found here. This is a fast-moving predator. It does not have any eyes so it finds its prey by using other **senses**. The centipede kills its prey with poison from its two front legs.

Once you have finished searching, put the logs back exactly as you found them. Look carefully at the leaves growing on plants. A common bug found on leaves is the aphid, or green fly. Aphids suck the sugary **sap** out of the veins of leaves. Aphids are eaten by ladybirds and their **larvae**.

In summer, collect the aphids and ladybirds living on the branch of a tree by shaking the branch over a white sheet. Quickly count the number of aphids on the sheet. Get someone else to count the ladybirds and their larvae. When you have finished counting, shake the sheet to let the animals go.

Show the number of ladybirds (the predators) and aphids (the prey) you have counted in a pyramid as on page 11.

▲ *A ladybird larva eating aphids.*

▼ *Shake the branches or knock the tree gently to let the animals fall on to the sheet below.*

Spreading seeds

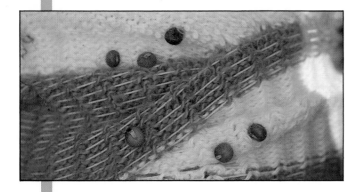

▲ *Find out which of the seeds attaches to your clothes.*

The fruits of plants hold seeds. These seeds will fall to the ground and grow into plants the next year. In autumn, the seeds are spread around the forest. Some are taken away by getting caught in animals' fur, while others fly through the air blown by the wind. The seeds of water plants may float downstream and develop in a place far from where they came from.

You can find out how seeds are spread. In woodland, collect the seeds of common cleavers. These seeds have little hooks on them. Also find some thistle seeds – they have a little silky 'parachute'. Look for some meadowsweet seeds which can often be found near streams and rivers.

▲ *Common cleavers is a straggly plant with prickly fruits.*

18

When you get back to the classroom, try and answer the following questions about your seeds:

1. Do they stick to your clothes?
2. Do they float in water?
3. Are they easily blown by air?
4. Do they stick to a feather?

Fill in a table like the one below on the right. If the seeds stick to your clothes you might think that the seeds could be spread by an animal. If they float on water, perhaps they could be carried downstream. From what you know about your seeds, try and decide how each kind of seed would be **dispersed** in woodland.

▶ *Make a table like this one for your results.*

▲ *Thistle seeds and meadowsweet seeds.*

	Common cleavers	Thistle seeds	Meadow sweet seeds
1.	✓		
2.			
3.			
4.			

Winter buds

A bud is a small shoot on a stem which will grow into a leaf or flower. The young leaves and flowers develop inside the bud during the winter. In spring the buds burst and the young leaves and flowers appear.

▲ *The flowers and leaves have burst from this horse chestnut bud. Can you see the brown scales?*

If you look at a twig or branch, you may see the places where last year's end buds grew from. This is because when the flowers or leaves fall off, they leave a girdle scar on the twig. The scar is made up of tiny thin lines around the twig.

▼ *A winter twig of horse chestnut.*

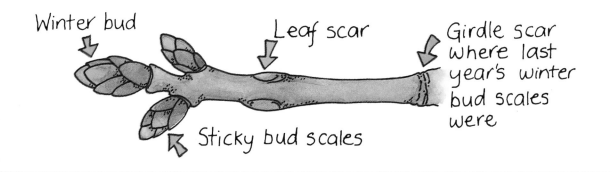

Winter bud

Leaf scar

Girdle scar where last year's winter bud scales were

Sticky bud scales

You can find out about the growth of winter twigs. You will need to collect at least twenty horse chestnut twigs in March while they are still in bud. Divide the twigs into two sets of ten. Stand each set in a separate jar of water. Put one set on a windowsill indoors where it is warm. Put the other set outdoors where it is cooler.

For one month, compare the growth of the two sets of twigs. Do this by drawing around each twig every four days on a piece of card. Your drawings will begin to show how each twig grows. Draw in the leaves and the buds as they burst. In this way you can make a record of how the twigs change.

Why do you think the two sets of twigs changed differently?

▲ The flowers of this horse chestnut are in full bloom.

▼ The children are drawing around winter twigs.

Growth of winter twigs

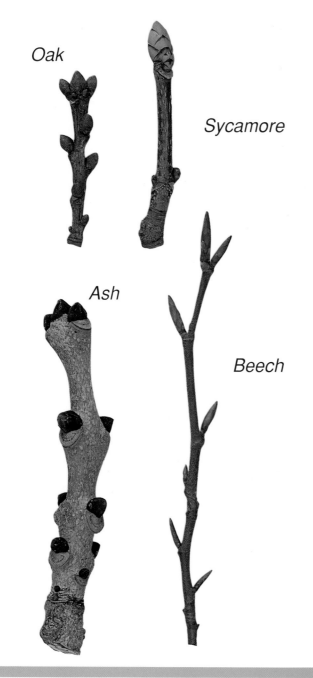

Oak

Sycamore

Ash

Beech

Some types of trees in woodlands grow faster than others. You can compare how fast different trees in woodland areas grow by collecting five winter twigs from each of the following trees: sycamore, oak, beech and ash.

Start with the ash twigs. Find the sooty-black bud on the end of each twig. Very carefully look back along the twig. You should be able to find the first girdle scar. The distance between the bud and the girdle scar tells you how much that twig grew last year.

Now find the girdle scar on each ash twig.

◄ *The growth of four winter twigs in one year.*

Make a bar line graph of all your ash twigs. First, lay a twig on your graph paper. Make sure that the girdle scar is level with the base line. Now make a mark on the graph paper where the end bud lies.

Take the twig away. Now draw a straight line between the mark and the base line. Do this with all five twigs from the ash tree. Make the same bar charts for all your other twigs.

Compare your bar line graphs once they are complete. Do they tell you that the trees grew at different rates? If so, which tree grew the fastest last year? Which tree grew the slowest? Did all the ash twigs grow exactly the same amount? Why use five twigs from each tree and not just one?

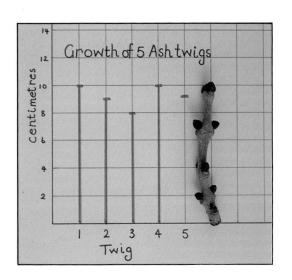

▲ *Your bar line graph should look like this.*

▼ *The growth of twigs varies a lot, even from the same tree.*

Growth rings

Each year the trunk of a tree gets thicker. This is because a new ring of wood is formed around the trunk. This new growth ring is just under the bark. Growth rings have two parts to them. There is a wider ring which is light in colour. This ring is formed in the spring. Another ring is formed in the summer of the same year. This is a much thinner and darker ring.

When a tree has been cut down you can find out how old it is by counting the rings. It is easiest to count just the number of dark rings there are. If you like, you can mark the ring which grew the year you were born, with a pin and a little flag.

Try to count how old these branches were when they were cut.

Look at the photograph on the right showing the growth rings of a tree. Start at the centre and count outwards until you find the fourth growth ring. Measure the thickness of the dark and light ring together. Now carry on counting until you find the ninth ring. Measure this ring also.

Did the tree grow faster in the fourth or ninth year?

▲ *Measure the thickness of the fourth and ninth growth rings.*

▼ *These children are flagging a tree trunk.*

Green dust

Look carefully at the trunk of the tree in the picture. Do you notice that one side looks greener than the other? Find a tree that is like this. Rub your finger on the green side of the tree. You will get some green dust on your finger. This dust is made up of many thousands of tiny green plants. These plants are called **algae**, and grow on the bark.

Find out if the algae always grow on the same side of tree trunks. You will need to know whether the side with the algae faces north, south, east or west. Draw a compass rose on some card, like the one in the picture on the next page.

◀ In this picture, the algae only grow on one side of the tree.

Put your compass in the middle of the rose that you have made. Make sure that north on the compass is lined up with north on the card by slowly turning the card. Stop when the compass needle is pointing to north on the card.

In the woodland, walk around your chosen tree. Your compass will show you the direction the algae on the tree is facing. Draw an outline of where the algae lies on your compass rose. Do this for at least ten trees.

Where does the algae mainly grow? Does it grow on the north, south, east or west facing part of the trunk? Why do you think this is?

▶ *These children are making their chart.*

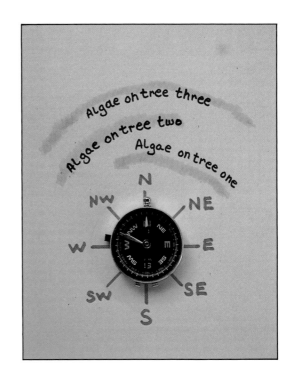

▲ *This is how to set your compass up and record where the algae grow.*

Mini woodlands

The flowers of the dog's mercury (left) are tiny and green. The flowers of the wood anemone (right) are large and white.

Warning: Dog's mercury and wood anemone are both poisonous. So look, but don't touch.

In the past, woodland was cleared to make way for fields. Long strips of woodland shrubs were sometimes left between fields to form hedges. Because these hedges are all that are left of the woodland, ecologists call them woodland 'ghosts'. These hedges are really mini woodlands and are very important for wildlife.

It is very exciting to go out into the country with your class to look for woodland ghosts. Look for the herbs in the hedge that once grew all over the woodland.

If you look in spring, you are likely to find wood anemone, dog's mercury and bluebells in flower.

Look for these plants in other places too. You may even find them on the edges of your school grounds. If you do find these plants, it is almost certain that woodland once stood there.

▼ *Look at the picture. Can you think of any reasons why farmers need hedges?*

▲ *The bottom of a hedge in early spring. Can you see what flowers are growing here?*

GLOSSARY

Acidic An acid is a sour chemical substance. Lemons are acidic.

Algae Simple plants that are able to make their own food.

Bacteria Microscopic living things that can make dead plants and animals rot away in the earth.

Birds of prey The species of birds that hunt other animals for food.

Canopy The top branches of trees in woodland.

Dispersed When seeds or fruits are scattered.

Food chain The feeding link between plants and animals.

Fungi Simple plants that cannot make their own food.

They have to live off dead matter or other living things.

Herbs Plants that die back to the ground each year.

Larvae The young of certain insects.

Nutrients Chemicals that plants need for healthy growth.

Predators Animals that kill and eat other animals.

Prey Animals that are killed and eaten by other animals.

Sap Sugary liquid in the veins of plants.

Senses The means by which living things can see, hear, smell, touch or taste.

Serpentine Wriggly like a serpent or snake.

BOOKS TO READ

Boulton, C. **Trees** (Franklin Watts, 1984)

Bown, D. **Wood** (Wayland, 1989)

Jennings, T. **Trees** (OUP, 1981)

Lucht. I. **Forest Calendar** (A & C Black, 1988)

McKenzie, S. **In the Woods** (Wayland, 1985)

Penny, M. **The Food Chain** (Wayland, 1987)

NOTES

This book involves learning about ecology through practical activities in woodland and is a suitable reference for use in the classroom. It is recommended that the activities for children in woodland should only be carried out under the supervision of a teacher.

p4-5 A geological map of your area will give clues as to the type of soil found around your school, in the garden and the local wood. Geological maps can be obtained from the Geological Museum in London.

p6-7 Children should be encouraged to make accurate observations. For example, most leaves are green, but vary enormously in their particular shade of green. If the leaf cannot be identified with the leaf description cards, children will have to add more of their own observations.

p8-9 It is important for children to understand that plants can make their own food whereas animals have to obtain their food. Through the food chain, green plants are the ultimate source of food for all animals, including top predators.

p10-11 Adult blue tits feed their young every $1\frac{1}{2}$-2 minutes for about 15 hours a day. The chart made should be pyramid-shaped. Most ecological pyramids of numbers are like this. If the feeding frequency is lower, ask the children to calculate from their 30 minute data how many caterpillars would have been fed in one hour and construct a pyramid from that. Arranging the data into sets of ten may make the pyramid easier to draw but is by no means essential.

p12-13 After the April count, get the children to formulate a hypothesis for what they will discover in July, eg. the number of mined leaves will increase. The investigation can be a data-gathering exercise to support such a hypothesis. The number of mined leaves will probably increase because there will be a greater number of moths laying eggs. The number of caterpillars will therefore increase.

p14-15 Pine needles rot very slowly because they are very acidic so the bacteria and fungi find it difficult to decompose them. You could get the children to look for pine needles on the floor of woodland. Some may have lain there for ten years or so.

p16-17 It is probably easiest to construct a pyramid of numbers if the data is arranged in sets of ten.

p18-19 The children will discover that there are many ways of dispersing seeds. They should understand that if plants grow too close together they will become overcrowded and weak.

p20-21 The twigs in the warm room will develop faster than the twigs outside. The children should be aware that for a fair test all other conditions should be kept constant. The children should suggest what other variables might affect the result eg. rain, wind.

p22-3 Almost certainly the oak trees grow the slowest and the others will vary. There will be a wide variation in the ash twigs, so the children should understand that there can be variation among one species. General statements in science should be based on as much data as possible. The children should realize that five twigs are a very small number to use for such an experiment.

p24-5 All things that grow do so faster in the early years. The growth ring of the fourth year is wider than that of the ninth year. The pattern of growth should be the same for all trees. This theory could be tested on other species of tree.

p26-7 The green single-celled algae are called pleurococcus. It is damaged by heat and strong light and so grows on the shady side of trees.

p28-9 Where the children find dog's mercury and wood anemone growing, get the children to look at old maps for evidence of woodland.

INDEX

The photograph on page 19 is by Deni Bown.

Thanks to the staff and pupils of Church Wood Primary School, St Leonard's-on-Sea, East Sussex, for their help in the compilation of this book.